Let's Get Cooking
PASTA

Over **100** tasty dishes

igloobooks

igloobooks

Published in 2017
by Igloo Books Ltd
Cottage Farm
Sywell
NN6 0BJ
www.igloobooks.com

Designed by Nicholas Gage
Edited by Jasmin Peppiatt

Food photography and recipe development
© Stockfood, The Food Media Agency
Additional imagery © iStock / Getty Images
Cover images: © iStock / Getty Images

LEO002 0417
2 4 6 8 10 9 7 5 3 1
ISBN 978-1-78670-863-2

Printed and manufactured in China

Contents

Meat Dishes

SERVES: **4** | PREP TIME: **15 MINS** | COOKING TIME: **30 MINS**

Chicken Pasta Salad with Cheese Crouton

2 chicken breasts, skin on
1 red pepper, deseeded and chopped
2 tbsp olive oil
300 g / 10 oz / 1 ½ cups fusilli pasta
½ lemon, juiced
handful black olives
4 slices baguette, 1 cm / ½ in thick
60 g / 2 oz / ½ cup goats' cheese log, sliced
mixed salad, to serve

1. Preheat the oven to 200°C / 400F / gas 6. Place the chicken and pepper in a roasting tin and drizzle with 1 tbsp oil and season. Roast for about 25 minutes or until the chicken is cooked through.
2. Leave the chicken to cool slightly in the pan, then tear into shreds and place in a bowl with the pepper and olives. Squeeze over a little lemon juice.
3. Meanwhile cook the pasta in boiling salted water according to packet instructions.
4. Drain and toss with a little olive oil to prevent sticking then tip into the bowl with the chicken.
5. Drizzle with the remaining extra virgin olive oil and season carefully. You may want more lemon juice.
6. Toast the baguettes brushed with a little oil under a hot grill until lightly gold.
7. Top with the goats' cheese and grill again until the cheese is bubbling.
8. Serve with the chicken pasta salad and some mixed leaves on the side.

SERVES: **4-6** | PREP TIME: **2 HOURS** | COOKING TIME: **50 MINS**

Lasagne

150 ml / 5 fl. oz / ⅔ cup beef stock
12 lasagne sheets
2 tbsp Parmesan, grated

FOR THE TOMATO SAUCE
1 tbsp olive oil
1 onion, peeled and finely chopped
2 celery stalks, finely chopped
2 cloves garlic, finely chopped
2 carrots, peeled and thickly sliced

2 courgettes (zucchini), thickly sliced
120 g / 4 oz / ½ cup pancetta, cubed
500 g / 1 lb / 2 ¼ cups minced beef
120 ml / 4 fl. oz / ½ cup white wine
800 g / 1 ¾ lbs oz / 4 cups tomatoes
550 ml / 1 pint / 2 cups beef stock

FOR THE BÉCHAMEL SAUCE
2 tbsp butter
2 tbsp plain (all-purpose) flour
700 ml / 1 ¼ pints / 2 ¾ cups milk
1 bay leaf
nutmeg, grated

1. To make the tomato sauce, fry the chopped vegetables, carrots, courgettes and pancetta in oil for 10 minutes.
2. Add the beef, breaking it up with a wooden spoon until fully cooked through then season with salt and pepper.
3. Add the wine and tomatoes and leave to simmer for 2 hours, adding more stock as it absorbs.
4. Heat the butter in a pan, then stir in the flour to make a roux. Whisk in the milk a little at a time.
5. Add the bay leaf and simmer for 10 minutes, whisking frequently until thick. Season and add grated nutmeg.
6. Preheat the oven to 190°C (170° fan) / 375F / gas 5. Add 4 sheets of lasagne to a baking dish and add a third of the Bolognese sauce in the bottom of a baking dish, then a quarter of the béchamel.
7. Repeat twice more, then cover the top layer of lasagne with béchamel and sprinkle over the parmesan.
8. Bake in the oven for 40 minutes until the pasta is tender. Leave to rest for 10 minutes before serving.

Tagliatelle Carbonara

500 g / 1 lb 2 oz/ 2 cups tagliatelle
2 tbsp butter
12 slices pancetta, chopped
4 egg yolks
100 ml / 3 ½ fl. oz / ½ cup double
   (heavy) cream
2 tbsp Parmesan, grated

1. Cook the pasta in boiling salted water according to packet instructions.
2. Heat the butter in a pan and fry the pancetta until golden.
3. Whisk the egg yolks and Parmesan into the cream.
4. Drain the pasta, return to the pan and, working quickly, scrape the pancetta and butter into the pan and toss.
5. Toss off the heat with the egg / cream mixture then serve immediately.

Ham Cannelloni

FOR THE FILLING
130 g / 4 ½ oz / ½ cup ham, chopped
400 g / 13 ½ oz / 1 ½ cups ricotta
2 tbsp Parmesan, grated
salt and pepper
12 cannelloni tubes or 12 sheets lasagne

FOR THE TOMATO SAUCE
2 tbsp olive oil
1 clove of garlic, chopped
800 g / 1 lb 12 oz canned chopped
   tomatoes
½ bunch basil, chopped
2 mozzarella balls, sliced

1. Preheat the oven to 180°C (160° fan) / 350F / gas 4. Mix the ham, cheeses and seasoning together in a bowl.
2. Spoon into the tubes or onto the lasagne sheets and roll up to make 12 cylinders, then lay in a greased baking dish.
3. Heat the oil in a pan and add the garlic and tomatoes. Leave to simmer, topped up with ½ a can of water, for 10 minutes, then add the basil and season. Spoon over the cannelloni.
4. Lay the slices of mozzarella over the top and drizzle with olive oil then bake for 15 minutes until bubbling.

SERVES: 4 | PREP TIME: 1 HOUR 15 MINS | COOKING TIME: 1 HOUR 40 MINS

Chicken Lasagne

150 ml / 5 fl. oz / ⅔ cup beef stock
12 lasagne sheets, pre-cooked
2 tbsp Parmesan, grated

FOR THE SAUCE
1 tbsp butter
1 tbsp olive oil
1 onion, peeled and finely chopped
2 celery stalks, finely chopped
2 cloves garlic, finely chopped
2 carrots, finely chopped

120 g / 4 oz / ½ cup pancetta, cubed
500 g / 1 lb chicken breast, chopped
120 ml / 4 fl. oz / ½ cup white wine
800 g / 1 ¾ lbs / 4 cups tomatoes

FOR THE BÉCHAMEL SAUCE
2 tbsp butter
2 tbsp plain (all purpose) flour
700 ml / 1 ¼ pints / 2 ¾ cups milk
1 bay leaf
nutmeg, grated

1. To make the tomato sauce, heat the butter with a little oil in a pan and add the finely chopped vegetables and pancetta and cook for about 10 minutes.
2. Add the chicken and cook until golden. Season with salt and pepper. Add the wine and tomatoes and simmer for about 45 minutes.
3. Make the béchamel by heating the butter in a pan until foaming, then stirring in the flour to make a paste.
4. Whisk in the milk a little at a time. Add the bay leaf and simmer for 10 minutes, whisking frequently until thick. Season and add a little freshly grated nutmeg.
5. Preheat the oven to 190°C (170° fan) / 375F / gas 5. Lay 4 lasagne sheets followed by a third of the Bolognese sauce in the bottom of a baking dish, then a quarter of the béchamel. Repeat twice more, then cover the top layer with béchamel and sprinkle over the Parmesan.
6. Bake in the oven for 40 minutes. Leave to rest for 10 minutes before serving.

Fusilli with Bacon

500g / 1 lb / 2 cups fusilli pasta
60g / 2 oz / ¼ cup butter
80g / 3 oz / ⅓ cup diced pancetta or
  smoked bacon
½ bunch tarragon leaves, chopped
salt and pepper

1. Cook the pasta in boiling salted water for 10 minutes or according to packet instructions.
2. Drain, reserving a little of the cooking water.
3. Meanwhile cook the pancetta in the butter until golden.
4. Throw in the tarragon leaves and 2 tbsp cooking water, then toss with the pasta.
5. Season with salt and pepper then serve.

Tagliatelle with Grilled Chicken

2 chicken breasts
1 courgette (zucchini), sliced
1 red pepper, deseeded and sliced
  into strips
1 tbsp olive oil
500 g / 1 lb 2 oz / 2 cups fresh
  tagliatelle
250 ml / 9 fl. oz / 1 cup double
  (heavy) cream
small handful thyme leaves

1. Cut the chicken into strips and toss it with the vegetables and oil and season.
2. Heat a griddle pan until smoking and griddle the chicken and vegetables until tender and cooked through.
3. Meanwhile cook the pasta in boiling salted water according to packet instructions. Drain and toss with a little oil and keep warm.
4. Warm the cream with a little salt and pepper and the thyme leaves.
5. Add the pasta to the cream then serve on plates. Spoon over the griddled chicken and vegetables.

SERVES: **4** | PREP TIME: **5 MINS** | COOKING TIME: **35 MINS**

Parma Ham Pasta Parcels

200g / 7 oz / 2 cups penne pasta
8 slices Parma ham
1 tbsp olive oil

FOR THE SAUCE
1 onion, peeled
2 cloves garlic, peeled
400g / 14 oz / 2 cups chopped
    tomatoes
2 tbsp basil

1. Cook the pasta in boiling salted water according to packet instructions. Drain, toss with a little olive oil and keep warm.
2. Mix the sauce ingredients in a blender until smooth.
3. Add 1 tbsp olive oil to a pan and add the sauce. Cook gently for around 20 minutes until the harsh onion taste has gone and the sauce has reduced a little. Adjust the seasoning.
4. Toss the pasta in the sauce.
5. Lay 2 slices of ham on each plate in a cross and spoon the pasta into the middle.
6. Fold the ends of the ham over the pasta to form a parcel.
7. Spoon a little extra sauce around to serve.

SERVES: **4** | PREP TIME: **20 MINS** | COOKING TIME: **20 MINS**

Spaghetti with Turkey

8 turkey escalopes
4 tbsp olive oil
1 courgette (zucchini), cut into batons
1 clove garlic, lightly crushed
4 sprigs thyme
400g / 13 ½ oz / 1 ½ cups spaghetti
4 tbsp pesto

1. Place the escalopes between 2 sheets of clingfilm and bat out until quite thin.
2. Heat the olive oil divided between 2 pans and sear the escalopes for 2 minutes on each side.
3. Remove from the pan and drain on kitchen paper. Add the courgette batons with the garlic and thyme and sauté until tender and golden.
4. Drain on kitchen paper.
5. Lay out the turkey escalopes and lay on a few slices of courgettes. Roll up and secure with a toothpick.
6. Cook the pasta in boiling salted water according to packet instructions.
7. Drain not too thoroughly and toss with the pesto – keep warm.
8. Return the escalopes to the pan. Cover with a lid and cook for another 3 minutes until the turkey is cooked through.
9. Serve with the spaghetti.

SERVES: **4** | PREP TIME: **10 MINS** | COOKING TIME: **14 MINS**

Orecchiette with Apples, Spinach and Parma Ham

500 g / 1 lb / 2 cups orecchiette pasta
2 tbsp butter
1 eating apple, peeled, quartered, cored and sliced
8 slices Parma ham, chopped
2 handfuls baby spinach leaves
2 tbsp pecorino, grated

1. Cook the pasta in boiling salted water according to packet instructions.
2. Meanwhile heat the butter and cook the apple until just tender but holding its shape.
3. Add the Parma ham and remove from the heat.
4. Drain the pasta, reserving some of the cooking water.
5. Toss the pasta with the apples and ham, adding a tbsp of cooking water to lubricate. Season with salt and pepper.
6. Toss through the spinach leaves, add the pecorino and serve.

Lasagne with Mushrooms

150 ml / 5 fl. oz / 2 / 3 cup beef stock
12 lasagne sheets
2 tbsp Parmesan, grated

FOR THE FILLING
1 tbsp butter
2 tbsp olive oil
1 onion, peeled and finely chopped
2 celery stalks, finely chopped
2 cloves garlic, finely chopped
2 carrots, finely chopped
200 g / 6 ½ oz / ¾ cup mushrooms

120 g / 4 oz / ½ cup pancetta, cubed
500 g / 1 lb / 2 cups minced beef
120 ml / 4 fl. oz / ½ cup white wine
800 g / 1 ¾ lbs / 4 cups tomatoes
450 ml / 1 pint / 2 cups beef stock

FOR THE BÉCHAMEL SAUCE
2 tbsp butter
2 tbsp plain (all-purpose) flour
700 ml / 1 ¼ pints / 2 ¾ cups milk
1 bay leaf
nutmeg, grated to taste

1. Heat the butter with a little oil in a pan and add the finely chopped
   vegetables, the mushrooms and pancetta and cook for about 10 minutes.
2. Add the beef, wine, tomatoes and half the stock, then lower the heat.
   Partially cover the pan and leave to simmer for 2 hours, adding more stock
   as it absorbs.
3. To make the béchamel, heat the butter in a pan then stir in the flour to make
   a paste. Whisk in the milk a little at a time. Add the bay leaf and simmer for
   10 minutes, whisking until thick. Season and add freshly grated nutmeg.
4. Preheat the oven to 190°C (170° fan) / 375F / gas 5. Add 4 lasagne sheets
   then a third of the filling in the bottom of a baking dish, then a quarter of
   the béchamel.
5. Repeat twice more, then cover the top with béchamel and sprinkle over
   the Parmesan. Bake in the oven for 40 minutes. Leave to rest for 10 minutes
   before serving.

SERVES: 6 | **PREP/MARINADE TIME: 12 HOURS 45 MINS** | **COOKING TIME: 3 HOURS 30 MINS**

Macaroni with Beef Stew

2 carrots, peeled and chopped
1 onion, peeled and chopped
1 onion, whole
1 cloves garlic, peeled
2 cloves garlic, peeled and chopped
1 bouquet garni
600 g / 1 lb 5 oz / 4 cups stewing beef, cubed
3 tbsp olive oil
2 cloves
125 g / 4 ½ oz / ¾ cup smoked bacon lardons
1 tbsp tomato puree
550 ml / 1 pint / 2 cups beef stock
500 g / 1 lb 2 oz / 4 ½ cups macaroni pasta

1. Combine the carrots, ½ onion and 1 garlic clove in a food processor. Peel the remaining onion, cut in half and push the cloves into it.
2. Place in a large bowl with the bouquet garni and the meat. Season and add 1 tbsp of oil and cover with film and leave to marinade overnight.
3. Remove the meat from the marinade, pat dry and fry in batches to seal all sides.
4. Return the meat plus the marinade to a casserole pan.
5. Add the lardons, garlic and onion and fry gently, stir in the tomato puree. Season and cook for 10 minutes.
6. Add the stock and turn up the heat until simmering. Cover and cook over a low heat for 3 hours.
7. Cook the pasta according to packet instructions. Drain and toss with a little butter to prevent sticking
8. Fish the cloved onion and bouquet garni out of the stew and serve with the pasta.

SERVES: **4-6** | PREP TIME: **1 HOUR 30 MINS** | COOKING TIME: **10-12 MINS**

Ravioli with Duck Liver and Mushrooms

FOR THE PASTA

500 g / 1 lb 2 oz / 2 cups '00' flour (Italian super-white flour)

6 eggs

FOR THE FILLING

3 tbsp butter

200 g / 7 oz / ¾ cup wild mushrooms, finely chopped

150 g / 5 oz / 2 / 3 cup field or flat mushrooms, finely chopped

½ onion, peeled and finely chopped

2 tbsp Parmesan, grated

1 tbsp flat leaf parsley, finely chopped

TO SERVE

4 thick slices duck liver pâté

100 g / 3 ½ oz / ½ cup mushrooms, thickly sliced

butter

Parmesan, grated

1. Combine the pasta ingredients and knead for 5 minutes. Cover with film and chill for 30 minutes.
2. Heat the butter in a pan and fry the mushrooms and onion. Stir in the Parmesan and parsley and season.
3. Using a pasta machine, roll out the dough as thin as possible, 10 cm / 4 in wide.
4. Place 1 tsp of filling in the middle of the sheet at one end. Repeat all the way along at 5 cm / 2 in intervals, then brush a little water around each filling in a circle.
5. Place another sheet of pasta on top then cut out the ravioli shapes. Heat 2 tbsp butter in a pan and cook the mushrooms.
6. In another pan, lightly salt the pâté slices and sear on each side for 30 seconds, then cook for 1 minute more.

Bring a pan of water to the boil and cook the ravioli for 4 minutes. Remove carefully then toss with butter and Parmesan. Serve immediately with the warm mushrooms scattered over and a slice of pâté on top.

Pappardelle with Ham

400 g / 14 oz / 3 ½ cups pappardelle
  pasta
6 slices of cured ham, such as Parma
2 bunches rocket
60 g / 2 oz / ½ stick cup butter
110 g / 4 oz / 1 cup Parmesan, grated
250 ml / 9 fl. oz / 1 cup crème fraiche
salt and pepper

1. Cook the pasta in a large pan of boiling salted water until al dente or just tender.
2. Drain and toss with a little olive oil to prevent sticking.
3. Cut the cured ham in half lengthways.
4. Roughly chop the rocket.
5. Heat the butter in a pan, add the pasta and stir. Sprinkle over the Parmesan then add the crème fraiche. Season and mix well.
6. Divide the pasta between 4 bowls and then lay the ham and rocket on top before serving.

Fusilli with Artichokes

500g / 1 lb / 2 cups fusilli pasta
2 tbsp olive oil
1 clove garlic, finely chopped
1 tbsp thyme leaves
300ml / 10 fl oz / 1 ¼ cups passata
285g / 10 oz / jar artichoke hearts,
  halved
1 tbsp, chopped

1. Cook the pasta in boiling salted water according to packet instructions.
2. Meanwhile heat the oil in a pan and gently fry the garlic with the thyme.
3. Add the passata and a splash of pasta cooking water and leave to simmer for 10 minutes.
4. Add the artichokes and season.
5. Drain the pasta and toss with the sauce.
6. Serve with the basil scattered on top.

Pasta with Artichokes and Serrano Ham

500g / 1 lb / 2 cups dried fusilli pasta
2 tbsp olive oil
1 clove garlic, chopped
285g / 10 oz / jar artichoke hearts, drained
4 slices Serrano ham

1. Cook the pasta in boiling salted water according to packet instructions. Save a small mug of the cooking water.
2. Meanwhile, heat the olive oil in a pan and gently fry the garlic.
3. Add the artichokes and ham and warm through.
4. Drain the pasta then toss in the pan with a little of the cooking water to amalgamate.
5. Serve sprinkled with Parmesan cheese.

Pasta, Cheese and Ham Frittata

300 g / 10 oz / 1 ¼ cps macaroni
4 thick slices ham, chopped
4 tbsp Parmesan or Gruyère, grated
3 sprigs thyme, leaves only
5 eggs, beaten

1. Preheat the oven to 180°C / 350F / gas 5.
2. Cook the pasta in boiling, salted water according to packet instructions.
3. Meanwhile whisk together the eggs, ham, cheese and thyme and season with salt and pepper.
4. Drain the pasta thoroughly then stir into the eggs.
5. Pour into a large oven proof frying pan and cook for about 20 minutes until the eggs are cooked through.
6. Serve warm or cold.

SERVES: **4** | PREP TIME: **15 MINS** | COOKING TIME: **30 MINS**

Fusilli with Marinated Lamb

300 g / 10 oz lamb fillet
2 tbsp raisins or sultanas
100 ml / 3 ½ fl oz / ½ cup Marsala
salt and pepper
500 g / 1 lb 2 oz / 2 cups fusilli pasta
1 tbsp butter
½ bunch basil
Parmesan, grated to serve

1. Slice the lamb into strips and marinate with the sultanas and Marsala for
   15 minutes.
2. Cook the pasta in boiling salted water according to packet instructions.
   Drain, toss with oil and keep warm.
3. Heat a frying pan until very hot, remove the lamb from marinade and pat dry,
   then fry briskly until still pink in the middle but coloured on the outside.
4. Add the marinade and sultanas to the pan and deglaze, reducing the liquid
   until syrupy.
5. Stir in the butter so the sauce is shiny.
6. Toss the pasta with the sauce and the lamb. Stir in the basil and serve
   with Parmesan.

Farfalle with Chicken and Vegetables

500 g / 1 lb / 2 cups farfalle
2 tbsp olive oil
1 onion, peeled and sliced
2 chicken breasts, chopped
140 g / 5 oz / ½ jar artichoke hearts
2 red peppers, 'cheeks' cut off
1 sprig oregano

1. Cook the pasta in boiling salted water according to packet instructions. Drain, reserving a little of the water.
2. Heat the oil in a pan and cook the onion for about 15 minutes until soft and sweet.
3. Add the chicken and peppers and cook briskly until golden.
4. Add the artichokes and oregano and season with salt and pepper.
5. Toss the pasta with the chicken, adding a little cooking water to lubricate.
6. Serve hot.

Tagliatelle with Beef and Cherry Tomatoes

300 g / 10 oz / 1 ¼ cups cherry tomatoes
2 beef steaks, sliced into strips
1 onion, chopped
1 tbsp olive oil
500 g / 1 lb / 2 cups tagliatelle
1 tbsp basil, chopped
2 tbsp Parmesan, grated to serve

1. Preheat the oven to 200°C / 400F / gas 6.
2. Place the cherry tomatoes, beef strips and chopped onions in a roasting tin and drizzle with oil. Season well and roast in the oven for at least 20 minutes or until well cooked.
3. Meanwhile cook the pasta in boiling salted water according to packet instructions
4. Drain the pasta.
5. Toss the pasta with the tomatoes and their roasting juices, the beef and the chopped basil.
6. Adjust the seasoning and serve with Parmesan.

Spirali Pasta with Parma Ham, Parmesan and Basil

500 g / 1 lb 2 oz / 2 cups spirali pasta
3 tbsp butter
4 slices Parma ham, cut into fine strips
4 tbsp Parmesan
1 tbsp basil, chopped

1. Cook the pasta in boiling salted water according to packet instructions. Drain, reserving a little of the cooking water and toss with a little oil.
2. Heat the butter in a pan and add the Parma ham.
3. Toss in the pasta and 2 tbsp water, then stir in the Parmesan and basil.
4. Season with salt and pepper and serve.

Linguine with Duck Liver Pâté and Mushrooms

500 g / 1 lb 2 oz / 2 cups linguine
4 thick slices duck liver pâté
100 g / 3 ½ oz / ½ cup mushrooms, thickly sliced
2 tbsp butter
Parmesan, grated

1. Cook the linguine in boiling salted water according to packet instructions.
2. Drain and toss with a little butter.
3. Heat the butter in a pan and cook the mushrooms. Season with salt and pepper and keep warm.
4. Heat a frying pan still quite hot. Lightly salt the liver slices and sear on each side for 30 seconds, then cook for 1 minute more. Remove from the pan.
5. Serve the linguine tossed with the mushrooms and their butter and Parmesan Top with a slice of pâté.

Conchiglie with Asparagus and Beef

500 g / 1 lb / 2 cups conchiglie pasta
8 stalks asparagus, woody ends
  snapped off and cut into short lengths
60 g / 2 oz / ¼ cup butter
1 clove garlic, sliced
¼ lemon, grated zest
8 slices air-dried beef, sliced into strips

1. Cook the pasta in boiling salted water according to packet instructions.
2. Add the asparagus 3 minutes before the end of the cooking time.
3. Meanwhile heat the butter and garlic in a pan, then add the beef and zest and toss together.
4. Drain the pasta, reserving a little of the water and toss with the butter sauce, adding 1-2 tbsp of reserved cooking water to amalgamate the sauce.
5. Season and serve.

Cannelloni Wrapped in Ham

3 tomatoes
500g / 1 lb / 2 cups ricotta
½ bunch basil, chopped
1 bunch chives, finely chopped
salt and pepper
12 cannelloni tubes
12 slices ham
olive oil

1. Plunge the tomatoes into boiling water and leave for 30 seconds. Remove and peel away the skin. Deseed and dice the flesh.
2. Mix the tomato concasse in a bowl with 1 tbsp olive oil, salt and pepper. Stir in the basil and chives and ricotta. Taste and adjust the seasoning, if necessary.
3. Cook the cannelloni tubes in boiling salted water for 10 minutes. Drain and pat dry.
4. Working quickly, use a teaspoon or piping bag to stuff the tubes with equal amounts of filling.
5. Wrap the tubes in a slice of ham and serve.

Tagliatelle with Duck Liver Pâté

4 thick slices duck liver pâté
250 g / 9 oz / 1 cup wild mushrooms
400 ml / 14 fl. oz / 1 ½ cups veal demi-glace (reduced veal stock)
salt and pepper
500 g / 1 lb 2 oz / 2 cups fresh tagliatelle
1 tbsp butter

1. Heat a frying pan until very hot and sear the duck liver pâté for 30 seconds on each side then leave to cook for 1 minute.
2. Remove to a plate and keep warm.
3. Add the mushrooms to the pan and fry briskly until the liquid evaporates.
4. Pour in the demi-glace and reduce by ⅓. Season and keep hot.
5. Cook the tagliatelle in boiling salted water according to packet instructions.
6. Drain and toss with the butter.
7. Serve with the duck liver pâté and mushrooms on top and the sauce spooned over.

Spaghetti and Bacon Fritters

200 g / 6 ½ oz / ¾ cup spaghetti
4 rashers bacon or pancetta, finely chopped
2 cloves garlic, finely chopped
1 tbsp parsley, finely chopped
2 eggs
1 additional egg yolk
3 tbsp Parmesan, grated
3 tbsp olive oil

1. Cook the pasta in boiling salted water according to packet instructions.
2. Cook the bacon in 1 tbsp of oil until golden.
3. Mix together the garlic, parsley, eggs and Parmesan, then stir in the bacon.
4. Drain the pasta and leave to cool, then roughly chop into shorter lengths.
5. Heat 2 tbsp oil in a pan (the bacon one for preference) and then spoon
   dollops of the spaghetti mixture into the pan.
6. Fry until golden and crisp on both sides. Serve hot.

SERVES: **4** | PREP TIME: **15 MINS** | COOKING TIME. **30 MINS**

Linguine Bolognese

500 g / 1 lb / 2 cups linguine

3 tbsp olive oil

2 onions, peeled and finely chopped

2 cloves garlic, peeled and finely chopped

1 pack pancetta or bacon lardons

500 g / 1 lb / 2 cups minced beef

800 g / 1 ¾ lbs / 4 cups chopped tomatoes

100 g / 3 ½ oz / ½ cup Parmesan, grated

2 tbsp parsley, chopped

1. Heat the oil in a pan and sweat the onion and garlic until soft.
2. Add the pancetta and fry until the fat runs.
3. Add the mince and break it up with a wooden spoon, stirring frequently until cooked.
4. Season with salt and pepper, then add the tomatoes.
5. Partially cover and simmer for 15 minutes.
6. Meanwhile cook the pasta in boiling salted water according to packet instructions.
7. Drain and toss with a little oil.
8. Stir the parsley through the sauce, then toss the pasta in the sauce.
9. Serve with grated Parmesan.

Fish Dishes

Pasta with Prawns and Coconut Milk

200 g / 6 ½ oz / ¾ cup spirali pasta
200 ml / 6 ¾ fl. oz / 1 cup coconut milk
1 stalk lemongrass, crushed
1 lime, grated zest
200 g / 7 oz / 2 / 3 cup raw prawns
    (shrimps), shelled
1 tbsp basil, chopped

1. Cook the pasta in boiling salted water according to packet instructions. Drain and toss with a little oil.
2. Meanwhile heat the coconut milk in a pan and add the lemongrass and lime zest and leave to simmer for 5 minutes to infuse.
3. Add the prawns and leave till they turn pink, then stir in the basil and season with salt and pepper.
4. Fish out the lemongrass stalk.
5. Toss through the pasta and serve.

Tagliatelle with Salmon and Sun-dried Tomatoes

500 g / 1 lb 2 oz fresh tagliatelle pasta
4 tbsp olive oil
200 g / 7 oz / ¾ cup smoked salmon
100 g / 3 ½ oz / ½ cup sun-dried
    tomatoes
1 tbsp chervil, chopped

1. Cook the tagliatelle in boiling salted water according to packet instructions.
2. Drain, reserving a small amount of the water, and toss with a half the olive oil.
3. Cut the salmon into strips and tear the tomatoes into pieces. Place in a bowl with the chopped chervil and the remaining oil.
4. Toss with the pasta, adding a little of the reserved water to lubricate the sauce.
5. Season with salt and pepper and serve.

SERVES: **4** | PREP TIME: **15 MINS** | COOKING TIME: **30 MINS**

Spaghetti with Mussels and Tomato

500 g / 1 lb / 2 cups spaghetti
500 g / 1 lb / 2 cups mussels, cleaned
2 tbsp olive oil
1 shallot, finely chopped
2 cloves garlic, sliced
pinch dried chilli flakes (optional)
400 g / 14 oz / 2 cups chopped tomatoes
1 tbsp basil, chopped

1. Cook the pasta in boiling salted water according to packet instructions. When cooked, drain and toss with a little oil.
2. Meanwhile place the mussels in a large pan with a splash of water and cook over a medium heat for 5 minutes or until the mussels have opened.
3. Drain in a colander over a bowl, then leave to cool.
4. Once cool, remove the mussel meat from the shells, reserving a few for decoration.
5. Heat the olive oil in a pan and cook the shallot and garlic gently. Add the chilli flakes if using.
6. Add the tomatoes and a splash of the mussel cooking liquor and leave to simmer for 10 minutes.
7. Add the mussels to the sauce then toss with the spaghetti. Stir in the basil, season and serve decorated with the reserved shells.

SERVES: **4** | PREP TIME: **10 MINS** | COOKING TIME: **15 MINS**

Linguine with Salmon and Courgettes

500 g / 1 lb 2 oz / 2 cups linguine
2 fillets smoked salmon, skin removed
2 courgettes (zucchini)
2 tbsp butter
200 ml / 7 fl. oz / ¾ cup double (heavy) cream
½ lemon, grated zest and juiced
1 tbsp basil, chopped

1. Cook the pasta in boiling salted water according to packet instructions.
   Drain and toss with a little oil and keep warm.
2. Meanwhile, gently flake the salmon into bite-size pieces.
3. Slice the courgettes lengthways then cut into ribbons with a vegetable peeler.
4. Heat the butter in a pan and cook the courgettes for 2-3 minutes until
   just tender.
5. Stir in the cream, lemon zest and juice, basil, and then the salmon,
   stirring carefully. Season with salt and pepper
6. Toss with the linguine and serve.

SERVES. **4** | PREP TIME: **1 HOUR** | COOKING TIMF: **5 MINS**

Ravioli with Creamy Lobster Sauce

500 g / 1lb 2 oz pasta dough

FOR THE FILLING
meat from 2 large crabs
200 g / 7 oz raw prawns
  (shrimps), shelled
75 ml / 3 fl. oz / ½ cup double
  (heavy) cream
1 tbsp chervil, chopped
1 egg, beaten

FOR THE SAUCE
800 ml / 1 pint 9 fl. oz lobster bisque
2 tomatoes, finely chopped
3 tbsp double (heavy) cream
½ lemon, juiced
handful chervil leaves

1. Place the prawns and cream in a food processor and blend to a puree. Mix with the crab meat and chervil.

2. Lay a sheet of pasta onto a floured work surface and place 1 tsp of the mixture at intervals along the sheet, leaving a 6 cm gap between each mound. Brush around each mound with a little beaten egg.

3. Top with the second sheet of pasta and press down lightly around each mound. Cut out or stamp out with a cutter and lay on a baking tray.

4. Heat the lobster bisque in a pan and allow to reduce to an intensity of flavour you like. Stir in the cream, tomatoes and a little lemon juice. Adjust the seasoning to taste.

5. Cook the ravioli in boiling salted water for 2 minutes until they float, then remove with a slotted spoon and drain on kitchen paper.

6. Serve with the hot sauce and garnish with chervil.

SERVES: **6** | PREP TIME: **30 MINS** | COOKING TIME: **50 MINS**

Seafood Lasagne

1 kg / 2 lbs / 4 cups mixed raw
  seafood
12 raw prawns (shrimps), shelled
12 sheets of lasagne, pre-cooked
5 tbsp olive oil
2 onions, peeled and chopped
1 tbsp butter
1 tbsp flour
400 ml / 13 ½ fl. oz / 1 ½ cups milk
1 bay leaf
nutmeg, grated to taste
pinch of cayenne pepper

1. Heat half the oil in a pan and add
   the onion, seafood and prawns.
   Cook gently for 10-15 minutes.
2. In another pan, heat the butter
   and when foaming, stir in the flour
   to make a paste.
3. Whisk in the milk a little at a time.
   Add the bay leaf and a little
   nutmeg then continue whisking
   for 10 minutes until the sauce is
   smooth and thick. Season well
   and add a pinch of cayenne.
4. Preheat the oven to 190°C
   (170° fan) / 375F / gas 5.
5. Lightly oil a baking dish and place
   4 lasagne sheets in the bottom.
6. Spoon over a third of the seafood,
   then some of the béchamel and
   repeat twice more, finishing with
   a layer of lasagne.
7. Pour over the remaining béchamel
   sauce and cook in the oven for
   about 30 minutes.
8. Leave to rest for 10 minutes
   before serving.

SERVES: **4** | PREP TIME: **5 MINS** | COOKING TIME: **12 MINS**

Farfalle with Scampi

500 g / 1 lb 2 oz / 2 cups farfalle pasta
2 tbsp butter
1 shallot, finely chopped
1 clove garlic, finely chopped
200 g / 7 oz cup raw shelled prawns
1 shot whisky
250 ml / 9 fl oz / 1 cup double (heavy) cream
salt and pepper
1 bunch chives, finely chopped

1. Cook the pasta in boiling salted water according to packet instructions.
   Drain and toss with a little oil.
2. Meanwhile heat the butter in a pan and sweat the shallow and garlic
   without colouring.
3. Add the prawns and fry briskly, adding the whisky and allowing it to evaporate.
4. Pour in the cream, season and cook until the prawns are just pink.
5. Toss the pasta with the sauce, sprinkling with chopped chives to serve.

Tagliatelle with Sea Urchins

500 g / 1 lb 2 oz / 2 cups tagliatelle
2 tbsp olive oil
2 shallots, finely chopped
2 cloves of garlic, finely sliced
100 g / 4 oz sea urchin meat
½ bunch parsley, chopped
juice of ½ lemon
salt and pepper

1. Cook the pasta in boiling salted water according to packet instructions.
2. Drain, reserving a little of the water and toss with oil.
3. Meanwhile, heat the oil in a pan and gently sweat the onion and garlic.
4. Add the sea urchin meat and parsley and toss well, then stir through the pasta and 2 tbsp cooking water.
5. Adjust the seasoning and squeeze over the lemon juice if desired.

Pasta with Pesto and Salmon

500 g / 1 lb / 2 cups penne pasta
2 tbsp olive oil
1 courgette (zucchini), thinly sliced
2 salmon steaks, cooked
handful black olives, pitted
  and chopped
2 tomatoes, finely chopped
4 tbsp pesto

1. Cook the pasta in boiling salted water according to packet instructions. Drain, reserving a little of the cooking water.
2. Meanwhile heat the oil in a pan and cook the courgette until tender.
3. Flake the salmon into large chunks and mix with the chopped olives and tomatoes. Stir in the courgettes.
4. Add to the pan with the drained pasta, the pesto and a little cooking water to loosen the sauce.
5. Season with salt and pepper and serve.

SERVES: 4 | PREP TIME: **15 MINS** | COOKING TIME: **15-20 MINS**

Seafood Spaghetti

500 g / 1 lb / 2 cups spaghetti
2 tbsp olive oil
1 shallot, finely chopped
2 cloves garlic, finely chopped
pinch dried chilli flakes
800 g / 1 ¾ lbs / 4 cups chopped tomatoes
2 sprigs thyme
200 g / 7 oz / 2 / 3 cup raw prawns (shrimps), shelled
8 scallops, sliced in half horizontally
250 g / 9 oz / 1 cup mussels, cleaned

1. Cook the pasta in boiling salted water according to packet instructions. Heat the oil in a pan and sweat the shallot and garlic with chilli flakes without colouring.
2. Add the tomatoes with a splash of water and simmer for 10 minutes. Drain the pasta and toss with a little oil.
3. Cook the mussels in a separate pan with a splash of water for 5 minutes until they have opened. Discard any that remain closed.
4. Drain over a bowl to catch the cooking juices. Remove the meat from the mussels once cool.
5. Add the thyme, prawns and scallops to the tomato mixture and leave to cook until the prawns are pink and the scallops just opaque.
6. Add the mussels and a little of their cooking juice and season. Toss the spaghetti through the sauce and serve.

Smoked Salmon and Pasta Salad

300 g / 10 ½ oz / 1 ¼ cups penne pasta
 or similar
200 g / 7 oz / ¾ cup smoked salmon
4 spring onions (scallions),
 finely chopped
4 tbsp watercress, chopped
6 tbsp extra virgin olive oil
1 lemon, grated zest and juice
cornichons, to decorate

1. Cook the pasta in boiling salted water according to packet instructions.
2. Drain, toss with a little oil and leave to cool.
3. Cut the salmon into fine strips and place in a bowl with onions and watercress. Add the pasta.
4. Whisk together the oil, lemon zest and juice and season.
5. Toss the salad with the dressing and serve immediately decorated with cornichons.

Tagliatelle with Tuna

500 g / 1 lb 2 oz / 2 cups tagliatelle
3 tbsp olive oil
3-4 red peppers, roughly chopped
salt and pepper
375 g / 13 oz cans tuna in olive oil,
 drained
½ bunch basil, chopped

1. Preheat the oven to 200°C (180° fan) / 400F / gas 6.
2. Roast the peppers in oil and seasoning for about 20 minutes or until soft and sweet.
3. Cook the pasta in boiling salted water according to packet instructions. Drain, reserving a little of the cooking water and tip into a bowl.
4. Toss with the roasted peppers, a little of the roasting juices and a tbsp of cooking water.
5. Flake in the tuna and basil and season then serve.

SERVES: 4 | **PREP TIME: 5 MINS** | **COOKING TIME: 20 MINS**

Linguine with Lobster

500 g / 1 lb / 2 cups linguine
2 tbsp butter
1 shallot, finely chopped
1 clove garlic, finely chopped
400 g / 14 oz / 2 cups chopped
 tomatoes
2 sprigs thyme
meat from 1 cooked lobster

1. Heat the butter in a pan and sweat the shallot and garlic without colouring.
2. Add the tomatoes with a splash of water and thyme and leave to simmer for 10 minutes.
3. Cook the pasta in boiling salted water according to packet instructions.
4. Drain and toss with a little oil.
5. Slice the lobster into chunks and toss through the sauce to heat up. Adjust the seasoning.
6. Toss the linguine with the sauce and serve.

SERVES: **4-6** | PREP TIME: **2 HOURS** | COOKING TIME: **3-4 MINS**

Salmon Pasta Triangles with Dill

FOR THE PASTA

500 g / 1 lb / 2 cups '00' flour (Italian super-white flour)

4 eggs

500 g / 1 lb / 2 cups spinach leaves wilted, squeezed dry and cooled

FOR THE FILLING

3 tbsp butter

1 shallot, peeled and finely chopped

200 g / 7 oz / 1 cup smoked salmon, chopped

100 g / 3 ½ oz / ½ cup ricotta

FOR THE SAUCE

250 ml / 9 fl. oz / 1 cup double (heavy) cream

1 tbsp dill, chopped

1. Place the flour in a bowl, add the eggs and the spinach and combine until the dough comes together. Remove from the bowl and knead for 5 minutes.

2. Cover with film and chill for 30 minutes. Heat the butter in a pan and sweat the onion until soft. Stir into the ricotta with the salmon and season. Leave to cool.

3. Remove the pasta from the fridge. Using a pasta machine, roll out the dough into one even sheet. Cut into 10 cm / 4 in squares.

4. Lay on a floured surface and place 1 tsp of filling in the middle of each square. Moisten the edges with a little water then fold one corner over to make a triangle.

5. To cook bring a large pan of salted water to the boil and cook for 3-4 minutes. Remove carefully with a slotted spoon and drain on kitchen paper.

6. Gently warm the cream with a little seasoning and the dill and serve over the pasta.

SERVES: **4** | PREP TIME: **10 MINS** | COOKING TIME: **35-40 MINS**

Seafood Minestrone

1 tbsp olive oil
1 onion, peeled and finely chopped
1 carrot, peeled and finely chopped
1 celery stalk, peeled and chopped
2 tomatoes, finely chopped
1 l / 2 pints / 4 ¼ cups chicken stock
50 g / 1 ½ oz / ⅕ cup macaroni pasta
750 g / 1 ¼ lb / 3 cups mixed raw seafood,
   such as prawns, scallops, mussels and squid
1 bunch parsley, chopped
½ lemon
salt and pepper

1. Heat the olive oil in a pan and sweat the onion, carrot and celery
   without colouring for 5 minutes.
2. Add the tomatoes and cook for a further 2 minutes.
3. Pour over the stock, bring to a simmer and add the pasta.
4. Cook for about 20 minutes until the pasta is tender.
5. Add the seafood and poach in the soup until the prawns turn pink,
   the scallops opaque and the mussels open. Discard any that remain closed.
6. Scatter over the parsley and adjust the seasoning.

Lumaconi with Salmon

500g / 1 lb / 2 cups lumaconi or other
  giant shell pasta
300ml / 10 fl oz / 1 ¼ cups double
  (heavy) cream
60g / 2 oz / ¼ cup salmon roe
¼ lemon, grated zest
1 tbsp chives, finely chopped

1. Cook the pasta in boiling salted water according to packet instructions.
2. Meanwhile heat the cream gently with the salmon roe, zest and chives.
3. Season with salt and pepper.
4. Drain the pasta and toss with the sauce gently. Serve.

Spinach Tagliatelle with Smoked Trout

500 g / 1 lb / 2 cups spinach tagliatelle
300 g / 10 oz / 1 ¼ cups smoked trout
1 pack rocket (arugula)
1 tbsp olive oil
Parmesan shavings

1. Cook the pasta in boiling salted water for 10 minutes or according to packet instructions.
2. Flake the trout and chop the rocket.
3. When cooked, drain the pasta, not too thoroughly, and toss with oil.
4. Stir through the trout and rocket, season and serve with Parmesan shavings.

SERVES: **6** | PREP TIME: **20 MINS** | COOKING TIME: **20 MINS**

Conchiglie Stuffed with Crab

1 kg / 2 lb 4 oz / 4 cups giant conchiglie shells
300 g / 10 ½ oz crab meat
2 large bunches basil, chopped
75 g / 3 oz / ⅓ cup pine nuts
5 cloves of garlic, chopped
extra virgin olive oil
3 tomatoes, finely chopped
100 ml / 3 ½ fl oz / ½ cup vegetable stock
salt and pepper

1. Cook the pasta in boiling salted water according to packet instructions. Drain and toss with olive oil.
2. Place the basil, garlic and pine nuts in a pestle and mortar and crush to make a paste then pour in enough oil to loosen.
3. Add the crab and tomatoes to the pesto and mix gently. Season.
4. Preheat the oven to 150°C (130° fan) / 300F / gas 2.
5. Stuff the pasta shells with the pesto mixture and place in a buttered baking dish.
6. Pour the stock into the bottom of the dish and cover with foil.
7. Bake for 10 minutes then serve.

Vegetable Dishes

Tomato and Pasta Soup

2 tbsp olive oil

1 onion, peeled and chopped

1 carrot, peeled and finely chopped

1 celery stalk, finely chopped

2 cloves of garlic, chopped

1 courgette, finely chopped

2 potatoes, peeled and finely chopped

400 g / 14 oz / 4 cups dried macaroni

2 slices Parma ham, chopped

400 g / 14 oz / 2 cups canned chopped tomatoes

1 dried red chilli, chopped

1 l / 1 pint 16 fl. oz / 4 cups chicken stock

salt and pepper

extra virgin olive oil

1. Cook the pasta in boiling water according to packet instructions.
2. Meanwhile, heat the oil in a pan and sweat the onion, carrot and celery without colouring.
3. Add the garlic and cook for 2 minutes until soft.
4. Add the courgettes and potatoes, stir well and leave to soften for a 5-10 minutes, then add the ham.
5. Pour in the tomatoes, crumble in a little of the chilli, then stir in the stock.
6. Bring to a simmer and leave to cook until the vegetables are tender – about 20 minutes.
7. Taste and adjust the seasoning if necessary, adding chilli if desired.
8. Roughly mash the vegetables with a potato masher.
9. Drain and mix the boiled pasta into the soup. Serve drizzled with olive oil.

SERVES: **4** | PREP TIME: **10 MINS** | COOKING TIME: **1 HOUR**

Tagliatelle with Green Vegetables

PASTA DOUGH
600 g / 1 lb 5 oz / 4 cups '00' flour (Italian super-white flour)
6 eggs or 12 egg yolks

FOR THE SAUCE
2 tbsp butter
200 g / 7 oz / 2 cups broad beans, double podded
200 g / 7 oz / 2 cups peas
8 asparagus stalks, woody ends snapped off and cut into short lengths
2 tbsp Parmesan, grated

1. Tip the flour into a bowl, make a well in the centre and crack the eggs into it. Beat the eggs till smooth then mix together with the flour as much as you can.
2. Flour your hands and bring the dough together into a ball. Remove from the bowl and knead for 10 minutes. Cover with film and chill for 30 minutes.
3. Roll the pasta out with a pasta machine to its thinnest setting, then use the tagliatelle setting to make the pasta shapes. Set aside, lightly dusted with flour.
4. Cook the beans and peas in boiling water for 4 minutes. Cook the pasta in boiling salted water for 4 minutes, save a small mug of the cooking water. Drain.
5. Heat the butter in a pan and add the vegetables. Cook for a few minutes then add a little of the pasta water.
6. Once the asparagus is tender, add the pasta and toss well to amalgamate.
7. Serve with Parmesan.

Tricolore Pasta Salad

400 g / 14 oz / 3 ½ cups farfalle
300 g / 10 ½ oz / 2 cups cherry
tomatoes
2 green peppers, roasted and cooled
1 ball buffalo mozzarella
1 tbsp basil, chopped
4 tbsp olive oil
2 tbsp red wine vinegar

1. Cook the pasta in boiling salted water according to packet instructions.
2. Drain and toss with olive oil.
3. Meanwhile tip the tomatoes into a bowl with the peppers and drizzle with the olive oil, the vinegar and season.
4. Toss the cooked pasta with the tomatoes and peppers, adding more oil if necessary to lubricate. Adjust the seasoning.
5. Tear over the mozzarella and serve.

Tagliatelle with Creamy Lemon Sauce

500 g / 1 lb 2 oz/ 2 cups fresh tagliatelle
250 ml / 9 fl. oz / 1 cup crème fraiche
1 lemon, grated zest and juiced
2 tbsp basil, chopped
salt and pepper

1. Cook the pasta in boiling salted water according to packet instructions.
2. Warm the crème fraiche in a pan with the lemon zest and juice, basil and season with salt and pepper.
3. Toss the pasta in the sauce with a little of the pasta cooking water to loosen.

SERVES: 4 | PREP TIME: 25 MINS | COOKING TIME: 25 MINS

Courgette Lasagne

4 courgettes (zucchini)
2 tbsp olive oil
2 cloves garlic, chopped
300 g / 10 oz / 1 cup ricotta
4 tbsp Parmesan, grated
½ lemon, grated zest
8 lasagne sheets
300 g / 10 oz / 1 ¼ cups crème fraiche
2 handfuls Cheddar, grated
1 ball mozzarella, sliced, optional

1. Preheat the oven to 180°C / 350F / gas 5. Grate 2 of the courgettes and slice the remaining 2 thinly lengthways using a vegetable peeler.
2. Heat the olive oil in a pan and fry the garlic until soft. Stir in the grated courgette and allow to soften. Fold into the ricotta and 3 tbsp Parmesan, then add the lemon zest and season well with salt and pepper.
3. Lay half the lasagne sheets in the bottom of a greased baking dish then spoon over half the filling. Place some of the courgette slices on top.
4. Top with the remaining lasagne sheets, then repeat until all the ingredients are used up, finishing with a layer of sliced courgettes.
5. Whisk together the crème fraiche, Cheddar and remaining Parmesan. Loosen with a little milk if necessary then spoon over the top of the lasagne.
6. Lay slices of the mozzarella over and bake in the oven for 20-25 minutes until bubbling.

SERVES: **6** | PREP TIME: **45 MINS** | RESTING TIME: **30 MINS** | COOKING TIME: **3 MINS**

Mushroom Ravioli

FOR THE PASTA
500 g / 1 lb 2 oz / 3 ⅓ cups '00' flour
6 eggs

FOR THE FILLING
3 tbsp butter
200 g / 7 oz / 2 ⅔ cup wild
  mushrooms, brushed clean
150 g / 5 oz / 2 cups flat mushrooms,
  finely chopped
½ onion, peeled and finely chopped
2 tbsp Parmesan, grated
1 tbsp flat leaf parsley, finely chopped
salt and pepper

GARNISH:
butter
Parmesan, grated

1. Place the flour in a bowl and make a well in the centre. Crack the eggs into the well.

2. Beat the eggs, then draw in the flour until the dough comes together. Knead the dough for 5 minutes. Cover with film and rest for 30 minutes in the refrigerator.

3. Heat the butter and sweat the onion and mushrooms. Stir in the Parmesan and parsley and season.

4. Using a pasta machine, roll the dough into sheets 2mm thick and around 10 cm wide. Lay on a floured surface.

5. Place 1 tsp of filling in the middle of the sheet at one end. Repeat all the way along at 5 cm intervals and then brush a little water in a circle, around each filling.

6. Place another sheet of pasta on top, then push the sheets together and around each mound of filling.

7. Cut the ravioli into shapes.

8. Bring a large pan of salted water to the boil and cook for 3-4 minutes. Remove carefully with a slotted spoon then toss with more butter and Parmesan to serve.

Spaghetti with Pesto and Garlic

500 g / 1 lb / 2 cups spaghetti

FOR THE PESTO SAUCE
small handful pine nuts
1 clove of garlic, peeled and chopped
3 big handfuls basil leaves, chopped
2 tbsp Parmesan, grated
extra virgin olive oil

1. Cook the pasta in boiling salted water according to packet instructions. Drain, reserving a little of the water.
2. Make the pesto sauce, whizz the ingredients in a food processor until you have a rough paste or pound in a pestle and mortar. Drizzle in enough oil to make a loose sauce.
3. Toss the pasta in the pesto, loosening with a little cooking water.
4. Serve with extra Parmesan.

Fettuccine with Rosemary Butter Sauce

500 g / 1 lb 2 oz / 2 cups fettuccine
  pasta
100 g / 3 ½ oz / ½ cup butter
3 sprigs rosemary leaves,
  finely chopped
2 cloves garlic, finely chopped
4 tbsp Parmesan, grated to serve

1. Cook the pasta in boiling salted water according to packet instructions.
2. Drain, reserving a little of the cooking water, and toss with a little oil to prevent sticking.
3. Meanwhile heat the butter in a pan and gently fry the garlic and rosemary until soft.
4. Toss the pasta in the butter with 2-3 tbsp of cooking water to emulsify the sauce.
5. Season and serve with grated Parmesan.

Angel Hair Pasta with Shallots and Parsley Sauce

500 g / 1 lb 2 oz / 2 cups angel
  hair pasta
4 tbsp butter
2 shallots, finely chopped
1 clove garlic, finely chopped
2 tbsp flat leaf parsley, finely chopped
4 tbsp Parmesan, grated

1. Cook the pasta in boiling salted water according to packet instructions.
2. Drain, toss with a little oil and keep warm.
3. Meanwhile, heat the butter in a pan and gently sweat the shallot and garlic without colouring.
4. Stir in the parsley, season and then toss with the pasta.
5. Serve with the Parmesan sprinkled over.

SERVES: 4 | PREP TIME: 5 MINS | COOKING TIME: 12 MINS

Spaghetti in Tomato Sauce

500 g / 1 lb 2 oz / 4 ½ cups dried spaghetti

2 tbsp olive oil

2 cloves garlic, chopped

400 g / 14 oz / 2 cups chopped tomatoes

2 tbsp butter

2 tbsp Parmesan, grated to serve

1. Cook the pasta in salted boiling water according to packet instructions. Drain and toss with a little extra virgin olive oil and keep warm.

2. Heat the oil in a pan with the garlic for a few minutes.

3. When the garlic starts to sizzle, increase the heat and throw in the tomatoes. Immediately place a lid on and leave for a few minutes till the crackling dies down.

4. Remove the lid, stir in the butter and season with salt and pepper.

5. Toss the spaghetti in the sauce and serve with grated Parmesan.

SERVES: **4** | PREP TIME: **2 HOURS** | COOKING TIME: **40 MINS**

Mushroom Lasagne

150ml / 5 fl oz / ⅔ cup vegetable stock
12 lasagne sheets
2 tbsp Parmesan, grated

FOR THE BOLOGNESE SAUCE
1 tbsp butter, 1 tbsp olive oil
1 onion, peeled and finely chopped
2 celery stalks, finely chopped
2 cloves garlic, finely chopped
2 carrots, finely chopped
120 g / 4 oz / ½ cup pancetta, cubed
500 g / 1 lb vegetarian mince
  substitute
120 ml / 4 fl. oz / ½ cup white wine
6 button mushrooms, finely chopped
400 g / 14 oz / 2 cups can tomatoes
450 ml / 1 pint / 2 cups vegetable
  stock

FOR THE BÉCHAMEL SAUCE
2 tbsp butter
2 tbsp plain (all purpose) flour
700 ml / 1 ¼ pints / 2 ¾ cups milk
1 bay leaf
nutmeg, grated

1. To make the sauce, heat the butter and oil in a pan, add the chopped vegetables and pancetta and cook for 10 minutes.
2. Add the vegetarian mince and the wine and stir for 5 minutes until it has been absorbed. Add the mushrooms so they blend in with the vegetarian mince.
3. Add the tomatoes and half the stock. Lower the heat and partially cover. Leave to simmer for 2 hours, adding more stock as it absorbs.
4. Meanwhile make the béchamel sauce: heat the butter in a pan and stir in the flour to make a paste.
5. Whisk in the milk, whisking until all the milk has been added.
6. Add the bay leaf and simmer for 10 minutes, whisking until thick and smooth. Add a little nutmeg.
7. Preheat the oven to 190C / 375F / gas 5. Add 4 lasagne sheets then spread a third of the Bolognese sauce in the bottom of a baking dish, then a quarter of the béchamel.
8. Repeat twice more, then cover the top layer of lasagne with béchamel and sprinkle over the parmesan.
9. Bake in the oven for about 40 minutes until the pasta is tender.
10. Leave to rest for 10 minutes before serving.

SERVES: **4-6** | PREP TIME: **1 HOUR 30 MINS** | COOKING TIME: **10 MINS**

Tortellini with Spinach and Cream

FOR THE PASTA
500 g / 1 lb 2 oz / 2 cups grade '00' flour
4 eggs
500 g / 1 lb 2 oz / 2 cups spinach leaves
  wilted, squeezed dry and cooled

FOR THE FILLING
3 tbsp butter
½ onion, peeled and finely chopped
1 clove garlic, finely chopped

500 g / 1 lb 2 oz / 2 cups spinach
  leaves
nutmeg, grated
100 g / 3 ½ oz / ½ cup ricotta
2 tbsp Parmesan, grated
1 tbsp flat leaf parsley, chopped

FOR THE SAUCE
250 ml / 9 fl. oz / 1 cup double cream
Parmesan, grated

1. Mix the pasta ingredients then knead with your hands for 5 minutes until
   smooth and elastic. Cover with film and chill for 30 minutes.
2. Heat the butter in a pan and sweat the onion and garlic .
3. Add the spinach, wilt down then add the nutmeg. Stir in the ricotta,
   Parmesan and parsley and leave to cool.
4. Using a pasta machine, roll out the dough into one even sheet. Cut into
   10 cm / 4 in squares.
5. Place 1 tsp of filling in the middle of each square, then fold one corner over
   to make a triangle.
6. Press the edges lightly together, bringing the corners of the triangle in
   together to make a circular shape.
7. To cook bring a large pan of salted water to the boil and cook for 3-4 minutes.
   Remove carefully with a slotted spoon and drain on kitchen paper.
8. Gently warm the cream with a little seasoning and serve over the pasta with
   grated Parmesan.

SERVES: **4** | PREP TIME: **10 MINS** | COOKING TIME: **30 MINS**

Spelt Pasta with Mediterranean Vegetables

500 g / 1 lb 2 oz / 2 cups spelt pasta shapes

2 tbsp olive oil

1 red onion, peeled and finely chopped

1 clove garlic, chopped

1 aubergine (eggplant), finely chopped

285 g / 10 oz / jar artichoke hearts, drained and halved

handful thyme leaves

250 ml / 9 fl. oz / 1 cup double (heavy) cream

2 tbsp Parmesan, grated to serve

1. Cook the pasta in boiling salted water according to packet instructions. Drain and toss with a little oil then keep warm.
2. Meanwhile heat the oil in a pan and fry the red onion very gently for about 15 minutes until very sweet and tender.
3. Add the garlic and aubergine and cook for about 10 minutes, seasoning lightly, until the aubergine is cooked.
4. Stir in the artichokes, thyme and cream and adjust the seasoning.
5. Toss the pasta with the sauce and serve with grated Parmesan.

Tortellini in Tomato Sauce

2 tbsp olive oil
1 onion, finely chopped
1 clove garlic, finely chopped
400 g / 14 oz / 2 cups chopped tomatoes
handful thyme leaves
500 g / 1 lb 2 oz / 2 cups ready made fresh tortellini,
  such as spinach and ricotta

1. Heat the oil in a pan and sweat the onion and garlic without colouring.
2. Add the tomatoes and a splash of water and simmer for 10 minutes, then
   stir in the thyme leaves and season.
3. Cook the pasta in boiling salted water according to packet instructions then
   drain well.
4. Toss the pasta with the sauce and serve.

SERVES: **4** | PREP TIME: **10 MINS** | COOKING TIME: **15-20 MINS**

Noodle Soup

1 tbsp olive oil
1 onion, peeled and finely chopped
1 celery stalk, finely chopped
1 carrot, peeled and finely chopped
1 clove of garlic, finely chopped
1 L / 2 pints / 5 cups chicken stock
80g / 3 oz / ¼ cup spaghetti
1 nutmeg
salt and pepper
2 tbsp Parmesan cheese, grated
extra virgin olive oil

1. Heat the olive oil in a pan.
2. Add the onion, celery and carrot and sweat until softened.
3. Add the garlic and cook for a further minute.
4. Pour in the stock and bring to a simmer.
5. Break the pasta into lots of small pieces.
6. Add the pasta and cook until 'al dente' or just tender.
7. Grate over a little nutmeg and adjust the seasoning.
8. Serve with Parmesan cheese and oil for drizzling.

SERVES: **4** | PREP TIME: **5 MINS** | COOKING TIME: **15 MINS**

Linguine with Peas and Watercress

500 g / 1 lb / 2 cups linguine
150 g / 5 oz / 2 / 3 cup peas
1 pack watercress, chopped
4 tbsp butter
½ lemon, juiced
4 tbsp Parmesan, grated

1. Cook the linguine in boiling salted water according to packet instructions.
2. 4 minutes from the end of cooking time add the peas.
3. When cooked, drain, reserving a little of the cooking water.
4. Melt the butter in a pan and wilt the watercress a little.
5. Toss in the pasta and peas with 1-2 tbsp of cooking water and season with salt and pepper.
6. Squeeze over a little lemon juice and serve with Parmesan.

SERVES: **4** | PREP TIME: **20 MINS** | COOKING TIME: **15 MINS**

Greens and Pasta Salad

400g / 14 oz / 3 ½ cups orechiette
pasta
1 courgette (zucchini)
1 fennel bulb, root trimmed
2 celery stalks, finely chopped
1 tbsp mint, chopped
1 tbsp basil, chopped
110 ml / 4 fl. oz / ½ cup olive oil
1 lemon, juiced

1. Cook the pasta in boiling salted water according to packet instructions.
2. Drain and toss with olive oil.
3. Meanwhile cut the courgette into small matchsticks and squeeze over a little lemon juice and salt to macerate.
4. Finely chop the fennel and add to the courgette, along with the celery and herbs and mix well.
5. Once the pasta is cooked, toss with the vegetables and add more oil to lubricate.
6. Season well and serve.

Penne with Green and Black Olives

500 g / 1 lb / 2 cups penne pasta
2 tbsp olive oil
1 clove garlic, finely sliced
800 g / 1 ¾ lbs / 4 cups chopped
   tomatoes
2 tbsp basil, whole leaves
1 handful mixed green and black olives
4 tbsp Parmesan, to serve

1. Cook the pasta in boiling salted water according to packet instructions.
2. Meanwhile heat the olive oil in a pan until quite hot, throw in the garlic and the tomatoes. Cover with a lid as it will spit.
3. When the spitting dies down, remove the lid and stir in the basil and olives, season and remove from the heat.
4. Drain the pasta and toss with the sauce.
5. Serve with grated Parmesan.

Ravioli with Mushrooms

2 tbsp olive oil
200g / 6 ½ oz / ¾ cup mushrooms,
   chopped
2 sprigs thyme
1 clove garlic, chopped
400g / 14 oz / 2 cups chopped
   tomatoes
500g / 1lb / 2 cups ready made fresh
   ravioli, such as wild mushroom
2 tbsp Parmesan, grated to serve

1. Heat the oil in a pan and add the mushrooms with the thyme and garlic.
2. Cook briskly until the liquid evaporates, season then add the tomatoes and a splash of water.
3. Simmer for 10 minutes.
4. Meanwhile cook the pasta in boiling salted water according to packet instructions.
5. Drain then toss with the sauce and serve with Parmesan.

Garlic and Parsley Spaghetti

400 g / 14 oz spaghetti
100 ml / 3 ½ fl. oz / ½ cup olive oil
2 tsp red pepper flakes
125 g / 4 ½ oz / 1 ½ cups sourdough or ciabatta breadcrumbs
4 cloves of garlic, finely chopped
2 tbsp flat-leaf parsley, finely chopped

1. Boil the pasta in salted water according to the packet instructions.
2. Meanwhile, heat the oil in a large sauté pan and fry the pepper flakes and breadcrumbs until they turn golden.
3. Add the garlic and parsley and continue to stir-fry until the breadcrumbs are crisp.
4. Reserve a cup of the pasta cooking water and drain the rest. Add two thirds of the breadcrumb mixture and toss to coat, adding a little of the cooking water if it looks too dry.
5. Divide between four warm bowls and top with the rest of the breadcrumb mixture.

SERVES: **4** | PREP TIME: **40 MINS** | COOKING TIME: **25 MINS**

Spinach Cannelloni with Tomato Sauce

12 cannelloni tubes or 12 sheets
  lasagne
handful Cheddar, grated

FOR THE FILLING
2 tbsp butter
olive oil
2 cloves garlic, chopped
Nutmeg, grated to taste
1 kg / 2 lb 4 oz spinach leaves, wilted
400 g / 14 oz ricotta
2 tbsp Parmesan, grated

FOR THE TOMATO SAUCE
2 tbsp olive oil
1 clove garlic, chopped
400 g / 14 oz / 2 cups chopped
  tomatoes
200 ml / 7 fl. oz / 1 cup water
1 tbsp basil, chopped

1. Preheat the oven to 180°C (160°
   fan) / 350F / gas 5.
2. Heat the butter in a pan with oil
   and cook the garlic for 2 minutes.
   Add the spinach and nutmeg
   and stir until the spinach is wilted.
3. Spoon into a sieve and press
   down firmly with a wooden
   spoon to extract as much liquid
   as possible. Once done, finely
   chop the spinach and leave to
   cool in a bowl.
4. Stir in the ricotta, Parmesan,
   seasoning and mix well.
5. Spoon into the tubes or onto
   the lasagne sheets and roll up
   to make 12 cylinders.
6. Place 2-3 of the tubes in each
   greased dish.
7. To make the tomato sauce, heat
   the oil in a pan and add the garlic
   and tomatoes. Leave to simmer,
   topped up with water, for 10
   minutes, then add the basil and
   season with salt and pepper.
8. Spoon the tomato sauce over
   the cannelloni in each dish,
   then sprinkle the Cheddar over
   the sauce and bake for around
   15 minutes until bubbling.

SERVES: **4** | PREP TIME: **25 MINS** | COOKING TIME: **2 MINS**

Faggottini with Basil

500 g / 1 lb recipe pasta rolled
  into 2 sheets

FOR THE FILLING
1 large bunch basil, chopped
200 g / 6 ½ oz / ¾ cup ricotta
1 tbsp olive oil
60 g / 2 oz / ⅓ cup butter
basil sprigs
½ lemon, grated zest

1. Stir the basil into the ricotta with
   a little oil and seasoning.
2. Lay a sheet of pasta onto a floured
   work surface and place
   teaspoonfuls of the mixture at
   intervals along the sheet, leaving
   a 5 cm / 2 in gap between each
   mound. Brush around each mound
   with a little beaten egg.
3. Top with the second sheet of pasta
   and press down lightly around each
   mound, pressing out all the air.
   Cut out or stamp out with a
   crinkled cutter and lay on a
   baking tray.
4. Repeat and then cover the ravioli
   with a damp tea towel until ready
   to cook.
5. Cook the ravioli in boiling salted
   water for 2 minutes, removing with
   a slotted spoon and drain on
   kitchen paper.
6. Toss gently with the melted butter
   and top with basil leaves and
   lemon zest.

Papardelle with Tomato Sauce

500 g / 1 lb / 2 cups papardelle pasta

FOR THE SAUCE
2 tbsp olive oil
1 onion, finely chopped
1 clove garlic, finely chopped
400 g / 14 oz / 2 cups chopped tomatoes
handful thyme leaves
3 tbsp ricotta

1. Heat the oil in a pan and sweat the onion and garlic without colouring.
2. Add the tomatoes with a splash of water and the thyme and leave to simmer for 10 minutes.
3. Cook the pasta in boiling salted water for 10 minutes or according to packet instructions, then drain.
4. Stir the ricotta into the tomato sauce then toss the pasta in the sauce.
5. Season with salt and pepper and serve.

Tagliatelle with Leeks

500g / 1 lb / 2 cups tagliatelle
3 tbsp butter
2 leeks, trimmed and finely sliced
2 sprigs thyme
300 ml / 10 fl. oz / 1 ¼ cups passata
salt and pepper

1. Cook the pasta in boiling salted water according to packet instructions.
2. Drain and toss with a little oil.
3. Meanwhile heat the butter in a pan and add the leeks and thyme with a little salt. Cook very gently until soft and sweet.
4. Add the passata and leave to simmer for 10 minutes.
5. Adjust the seasoning in the sauce, adding salt and pepper to taste.
6. Drain the pasta and toss with the sauce before serving.

SERVES: **4** | PREP TIME: **10 MINS** | COOKING TIME: **10 MINS**

Tagliatelle with Vegetables and Cream

500g / 1 lb / 2 cups tagliatelle
1 tbsp butter
1 shallot, finely chopped
1 clove of garlic, finely chopped
1 courgette, diced
1 red pepper, deseeded and diced
400ml / 13 ½ fl oz / 1 ½ cups double (heavy) cream or crème fraiche
salt and pepper
3 tbsp Parmesan, grated

1. Heat the butter in a pan and sweat the shallot and garlic without colouring.
2. Once softened, add the diced courgette and pepper and cook until tender.
3. Cook the pasta in boiling salted water according to packet instructions.
   Drain and toss with a little oil.
4. Add the cream to the vegetables and season well.
5. Toss the pasta with the cream sauce and serve with Parmesan.

SERVES: **4** | PREP TIME: **5 MINS** | COOKING TIME: **12 MINS**

Farfalle with Spicy Cherry Tomatoes

500 g / 1 lb / 2 cups farfalle pasta
2 tbsp olive oil
2 cloves garlic, finely chopped
1 tbsp sage leaves, chopped
300 g / 10 oz / 1 ¼ cups cherry
  tomatoes, halved
Tabasco, to taste

1. Cook the pasta in boiling salted water according to packet instructions.
2. Heat the olive oil in a pan and add the garlic and sage leaves. Fry the sage leaves until crisp, then remove from the pan and drain on kitchen paper.
3. Add the tomatoes and toss in the flavoured oil until just tender, then sprinkle with Tabasco to taste. Season with salt and pepper and remove from the heat.
4. Drain the pasta – not too thoroughly – then toss with the tomatoes and sage leaves.
5. Serve with more Tabasco if desired.

SERVES: **4** | PREP TIME: **15 MINS** | COOKING TIME: **35 MINS**

Maltagliata with Artichokes

12 lasagne sheets
4 globe artichokes, prepared in
 acidulated water
1 handful black olives
1 handful green olives
½ medium courgette, halved and
 thinly sliced
2 confit lemons, quartered
2 tbsp olive oil
salt and pepper

1. Using a non-iron or aluminium pan,
 boil the artichokes in salted,
 acidulated water for about 30
 minutes, or until one of the outer
 leaves pulls away easily.
2. Drain and cut into quarters.
3. Cut the lasagne sheets into
 irregular shapes (maltagliata means
 mal-formed in Italian).
4. Cook in boiling water according
 to packet instructions then drain.
5. Heat the oil in a pan with the
 confit lemons and gently warm
 the artichokes, olives and courgette
 slices through in the oil. Season
 with salt and pepper.
6. Toss with the pasta shapes
 and serve.

Penne with Chilli Tomato Sauce

500 g / 1lb / 2 cups penne pasta
2 tbsp olive oil
2 cloves garlic, chopped
1 red chilli, chopped
400 g / 14 oz / 2 cups chopped
 tomatoes
basil leaves

1. Cook the pasta according to packet instructions in boiling salted water.
2. Meanwhile heat the oil in a pan and gently fry the garlic and chilli.
3. Add the tomatoes, turn the heat up and bubble briskly for 10 minutes.
4. Drain the pasta and toss with the sauce then stir in the basil.
5. Serve hot.

Green Pesto Pasta Salad

500 g / 1 lb / 2 cups farfalle pasta
1 tbsp olive oil
6 tbsp green pesto
2 tbsp Parmesan, grated
salt and pepper

1. Cook the pasta in boiling, salted water according to packet instructions or until al dente.
2. Toss the pasta with the pesto and the olive oil and season to taste.
3. Serve sprinkled with Parmesan.

SERVES: 6 | PREP TIME: 25 MINS | COOKING TIME: 30 MINS

Wild Mushroom and Shallot Cannelloni

3 tbsp olive oil
2 shallots, finely chopped
1 onion, finely chopped
1 clove garlic, finely chopped
500 g / 1 lb 2 oz / 2 cups wild mushrooms
18 cannelloni tubes
4 tbsp parsley, chopped
100 ml / 3 ½ fl. oz / ½ cup double (heavy) cream
40 g / 1 ½ oz / ⅛ cup butter
3 tbsp Parmesan, grated

1. Preheat the oven to 200°C / 400F / gas 6.
2. Heat the oil in a casserole pan and add the shallot and onion. Cook for a few minutes, stirring regularly.
3. Add the mushrooms and garlic and cook until the liquid has evaporated. Season with salt and pepper, then add the parsley and cream.
4. Reduce until the cream has almost gone, then remove from the heat.
5. Cook the cannelloni tubes in boiling salted water according to packet instructions. Drain thoroughly and pat dry.
6. Stuff the cannelloni tubes with the mushroom mixture – either use a piping bag or a teaspoon.
7. Place in a buttered baking dish and sprinkle with parmesan and a few dots of butter.
8. Cook in the oven for 10 minutes then serve.

SERVES: **4-6** | PREP TIME: **40 MINS** | COOKING TIME: **30 MINS**

Lasagne with Romanesco Cauliflower

500 g / 1 lb 2 oz / 2 cups broccoli, separated into florets
500 g / 1 lb 2 oz / 2 cups romanesco cauliflower, separated into florets
3 tbsp olive oil
4 cloves garlic, finely chopped
1 tbsp thyme
6 anchovies, chopped
pinch dried chilli flakes
12 lasagne sheets
500 ml / 18 fl. oz / 2 cups ricotta
200 g / 7 oz / ¾ cup Parmesan, grated
200 g / 7 oz / ¾ cup mozzarella cheese

1. Preheat the oven to 190°C (170°) / 375F / gas 5. Boil the cauliflower and broccoli for 5 minutes, then drain, reserving the cooking water.
2. Heat 1 tbsp oil in a large pan and add the garlic, thyme, anchovies and chilli flakes. Allow the anchovies to melt, then stir in the florets and 5 tbsp of cooking water.
3. Cover partially with a lid and cook for 20 minutes until the vegetables are very tender. Lightly crush and season, then leave to cool. Lay 4 of the lasagne sheets in a buttered baking dish.
4. Stir the ricotta and half the Parmesan into the cooled vegetables then spread half over the pasta. Top with 4 sheets of pasta, repeat and finish with a layer of pasta.
5. Place the sliced mozzarella and Parmesan over the top of the pasta, drizzle with oil and bake for about 30 minutes, until bubbling and golden.
6. Serve hot or warm.

Tomato and Purple Basil Spaghetti

400 g / 14 oz spaghetti
100 ml / 3 ½ fl. oz / ½ cup olive oil
2 cloves of garlic, unpeeled and
   squashed
1 small bunch thyme, leaves only
200 g / 7 oz / 1 ½ cups cherry
   tomatoes, halved
1 large handful purple basil leaves

1. Boil the pasta in salted water according to the packet instructions or until al dente.
2. Meanwhile, heat the oil in a large sauté pan with the garlic. When it starts to sizzle, discard the garlic.
3. Stir in the thyme leaves and cook over a low heat for 1 minute. Add the cherry tomatoes and let them warm through.
4. Drain the pasta, then toss with the tomatoes and thyme in the sauté pan. Divide between four warm bowls and garnish with purple basil.

Spiral Pasta with Tomato and Basil

500 g / 1 lb / 2 cups spirali pasta
2 tbsp olive oil
1 clove garlic, finely sliced
800 g / 1 ¾ lbs / 4 cups chopped
   tomatoes
2 tbsp basil, roughly chopped
1 ball mozzarella

1. Cook the pasta in boiling salted water according to packet instructions.
2. Meanwhile heat the olive oil in a pan until quite hot, throw in the garlic and the tomatoes. Cover with a lid as it will spit.
3. When the spitting dies down, remove the lid and stir in the basil, season and remove from the heat.
4. Drain the pasta and toss with the sauce.
5. Stir in chunks of mozzarella and serve.

Raviolone with Artichokes

500g / 1 lb 2 oz /pasta dough, chilled

FOR THE FILLING
400g / 14 oz / 1 ½ cups Jerusalem
    artichokes
80g / 3 oz / ⅓ cup butter
2 tbsp cream
12 quail eggs

FOR THE SAUCE
4 tbsp butter
2 tsp black truffle juice
2 tomatoes, peeled, seeded and finely
    chopped
½ bunch chives, finely chopped

1. Boil the artichokes for 10 minutes in salted water. Drain then tip into a liquidizer with the butter, cream and seasoning and blend to a puree. Leave to cool.
2. Remove the pasta from the fridge. Using a pasta machine, roll out the dough into sheets about 1-2mm thick and 10 cm / 4 in wide.
3. Place 1 tsp of filling in the middle of the sheet at one end. Create a well in the centre and crack a quail's egg into the well.
4. Repeat all the way along at 5 cm / 2 in intervals, then brush water around each filling in a circle.
5. Place another sheet of pasta on top, then, working from one end to the other push the sheets together, around each mound of filling. Press down gently and cut the ravioli shapes.
6. Cook in boiling salted water, a few at a time, for 1 minute.
7. Heat the butter in a pan with 2 tsp of truffle juice.
8. Pour over the ravioli and decorate with tomatoes and chives.

SERVES: **4** | PREP TIME: **10 MINS** | COOKING TIME: **15 MINS**

Penne with Orange and Mushrooms

500 g / 1 lb 2 oz / 2 cups penne pasta
2 tbsp butter
olive oil
2 handfuls mixed wild mushrooms, torn
1 small orange, segmented
small handful sage leaves, chopped
salt and pepper
4 tbsp Parmesan, grated

1. Cook the pasta in boiling salted water according to packet instructions.
2. Drain, reserving a little of the water and toss with olive oil.
3. Meanwhile heat the butter in a pan and cook the mushrooms until the liquid has evaporated.
4. Add the orange segments and sage leaves and season.
5. Toss the pasta with the mushrooms and 2 tbsp cooking water.
6. Serve scattered generously with grated Parmesan.

Grilled Ravioli with Asparagus

500 g / 1lb 2 oz / 2 cups ready made fresh ravioli, spinach and ricotta

8 stalks asparagus, woody ends snapped off

200 g / 7 oz / ¾ cup Fontina cheese

1. Cook the pasta in boiling salted water according to packet instructions, then drain and toss with a little butter.
2. Cut the asparagus into short lengths and parboil in salted water for 3 minutes. Drain and pat dry.
3. Tip the ravioli and asparagus into a greased baking dish, season lightly and cover with slices of fontina.
4 Grill until bubbling.

Penne all'Arrabiata

500 g / 1 lb 2 oz / 2 cups penne pasta

2 tbsp olive oil

2 cloves garlic, chopped

1 red chilli, chopped

400 g / 14 oz / 2 cups chopped tomatoes

1 tbsp basil, chopped

1. Cook the pasta according to packet instructions in boiling salted water.
2. Meanwhile heat the oil in a pan and gently fry the garlic and chilli.
3. Add the tomatoes, turn the heat up and bubble briskly for 10 minutes.
4. Drain the pasta and toss with the sauce then stir in the basil.
5. Serve hot.

Cheese Dishes

SERVES: **4** | PREP TIME: **20 MINS** | COOKING TIME: **55 MINS**

Parmesan Pumpkin Pasta Bake

1 small butternut squash, peeled and cubed

2 tbsp olive oil

1 tbsp fresh thyme leaves

600 ml / 1 pint / 2 ½ cups milk

400 g / 14 oz / 4 cups dried macaroni

2 tbsp butter

1 ½ tbsp plain flour

150 g / 5 ½ oz / 1 ½ cups Cheddar cheese, grated

1. Preheat the oven to 190°C (170°C fan) / 375F / gas 5.
2. Toss the squash with the oil and thyme and season with salt and pepper. Spread it out in a large roasting tin and roast for 30 minutes, turning halfway through.
3. Transfer the squash to a liquidizer and blend with the milk until smooth.
4. Cook the macaroni in boiling, salted water for 10 minutes or until almost cooked. Drain well.
5. Meanwhile, pour the squash milk into a saucepan and add the butter and flour. Stir over a medium heat until it thickens and starts to simmer.
6. Take the pan off the heat and stir in the cheese. Stir in the macaroni and scrape it into a baking dish.
7. Bake for 45 minutes or until the top is golden brown and the pasta is cooked.

Macaroni with Blue Cheese Sauce

500 g / 1 lb / 2 cups macaroni pasta
1 tbsp butter
120 g / 4 ¼ oz / ½ cup mascarpone
100 g / 3 ½ oz / ½ cup Gorgonzola,
  piccante or dolce

1. Cook the pasta in boiling salted water according to packet instructions.
2. Drain and toss with a little butter.
3. Meanwhile heat the mascarpone with the Gorgonzola, stirring until it melts.
4. Season generously with black pepper.
5. Toss the pasta with the sauce and serve.

Penne with Courgette, Mint and Parmesan

400 g / 14 oz / 4 cups penne
100 ml / 3 ½ fl. oz / ½ cup olive oil
2 cloves of garlic, unpeeled and
  squashed
3 small courgettes (zucchini), thickly
  sliced
2 tbsp mint leaves, chopped, plus a few
  sprigs to garnish
75 g / 2 ½ oz / ¾ cup Parmesan,
  finely grated

1. Boil the pasta in salted water according to the packet instructions or until al dente.
2. Meanwhile, heat the oil in a large sauté pan with the garlic until it starts
   to sizzle, then discard the garlic.
3. Fry the courgettes for 4 minutes on each side or until golden brown, then
   stir in the mint and season with salt and pepper.
4. Drain the pasta and toss with the courgettes, then divide between four
   warm bowls. Scatter over the Parmesan and garnish with mint sprigs.

SERVES: **4** | PREP TIME: **15 MINS** | COOKING TIME: **12 MINS**

Pasta with Mussels in Gorgonzola Sauce

500 g / 1 lb 2 oz / 4 ½ cups farfalle pasta
1 tbsp butter
1 shallot, finely chopped
1 red pepper, deseeded and finely chopped
1 clove garlic, chopped
500 g / 1 lb 2 oz / 3 ⅓ cups mussels, cleaned
100 ml / 3 ½ fl. oz / ½ cup pastis
120 g / 4 ½ oz / ½ cup Gorgonzola
120 g / 4 ½ oz / ½ cup mascarpone

1. Cook the pasta in boiling salted water according to packet instructions. Once cooked, drain and toss with a little oil and keep warm.
2. Meanwhile heat the butter in a large pan and add the shallot, pepper and garlic.
3. Once softened add the mussels and pastis, allow to bubble up then cover with a lid and leave to simmer for about 5 minutes or until the mussels have opened.
4. Carefully tip the mussels into a colander over a large bowl to collect the cooking liquor, leaving any sediment behind in the bottom and discarding any mussels that remain closed.
5. Heat the Gorgonzola and mascarpone in a pan then add a little of the reserved cooking liquor and season with black pepper.
6. Remove the meat from most of the mussels and add to the pan with the pasta.
7. Serve decorated with remaining mussel shells.

SERVES: 4 | PREP TIME: **20 MINS** | COOKING TIME: **30 MINS**

Macaroni Cheese

250 g / 9 oz / 1 cup macaroni pasta
40 g / 1 ½ oz / ⅛ cup butter
40 g / 1 ½ oz / ⅛ cup flour
600 ml / 1 pint 2 fl. oz / 2 ½ cups milk
250 g / 9 oz / 1 cup Gruyère, grated
4 tbsp Parmesan, grated
4 slices good-quality ham,
  finely chopped
nutmeg, grated to taste

1. Preheat the oven to 180°C / 350F /
   gas 4. Cook the pasta in boiling
   salted water according to packet
   instructions. Drain and toss with
   a little oil to prevent sticking.
2. Meanwhile heat the butter in a pan
   and when foaming add the flour.
   Stir to form a paste, then whisk in
   the milk a little at a time.
3. Add all the milk, whisking
   constantly to ensure the sauce is
   smooth, then reduce the heat and
   cook out for 10 minutes, whisking
   every now and then to prevent the
   bottom catching.
4. Stir in the Gruyère, half the
   Parmesan, the ham and season
   with salt and pepper. Grate in a
   little nutmeg.
5. Stir the macaroni into the sauce
   then tip into a baking dish.
6. Scatter the Parmesan over the top
   and bake for 20-30 minutes until
   bubbling.

SERVES: **4** | PREP TIME: **40 MINS** | COOKING TIME: **30 MINS**

Ricotta Spinach Cannelloni

2 tbsp butter
1 tbsp olive oil
2 cloves garlic, chopped
nutmeg, grated to taste
1 kg / 2 lbs / 4 ½ cups spinach leaves
400g / 13 ½ oz / 1 ½ cups ricotta
2 tbsp Parmesan, grated
12 cannelloni tubes

FOR THE TOMATO SAUCE
2 tbsp olive oil
1 clove of garlic, chopped
2 x 400g can chopped tomatoes
½ bunch basil, chopped

1. Preheat the oven to 180C / 350F / gas 5. To make the filling, heat the butter in a large pan with the oil and cook the garlic for 2 minutes.
2. Add the spinach and nutmeg and stir and toss until the spinach is completely wilted.
3. Spoon into a sieve and press down firmly with a wooden spoon to extract as much liquid as possible. Once done, finely chop the spinach and leave to cool in a bowl.
4. Stir in the ricotta, Parmesan and seasoning and mix well.
5. Spoon into the tubes or onto the lasagne sheets and roll up to make 12 cylinders, then lay in a greased baking dish.
6. To make the tomato sauce, heat the oil in a pan and add the garlic and tomatoes. Leave to simmer, topped up with ½ a can of water, for 10 minutes, then add the basil and season.
7. Spoon over the cannelloni and bake for around 15 minutes until bubbling.

SERVES: **4-5** | PREP TIME: **15 MINS** | COOKING TIME: **35 MINS**

Penne Rigate with Béchamel

500 g / 1 lb 2 oz / 2 cups penne pasta
60 g / 2 oz / ¼ cup butter
30 g / 1 oz / ⅛ cup plain (all purpose) flour
400 ml / 14 fl. oz / 1 ¼ cups milk
nutmeg, grated to taste
6 tbsp Parmesan, grated

1. Cook the pasta in boiling salted water according to packet instructions. Drain and toss with a little olive oil and keep warm.
2. Preheat the oven to 220°C (200° fan) / 425F / gas 7.
3. Heat 2/3 of the butter in a pan and when foaming add the flour. Stir to make a paste and then pour in the milk a third at a time, whisking constantly to make a smooth béchamel sauce.
4. Leave to cook out for 10 minutes over a gentle heat, stirring well regularly. Season well and grate in a little nutmeg.
5. Butter a large gratin dish and tip in the pasta. Pour over the béchamel and fork through the pasta.
6. Scatter with Parmesan and a little extra butter. Place in the oven for 10-15 minutes until the top is golden and glazed.

SERVES: **6** | PREP TIME: **30 MINS** | COOKING TIME: **1 HOUR 15 MINS**

Feta and Artichoke Cannelloni

6 globe artichokes
1 lemon, juiced
4 tbsp olive oil
1 onion, peeled and chopped
2 cloves garlic, chopped
200 ml / 7 fl. oz / ⅘ cup white wine
12 sheets of lasagne pasta
200 g / 7 oz / 1 ⅓ cups feta
400 ml / 14 fl. oz / 2 cups passata
2 tbsp basil, chopped

1. Remove some of the tough outer leaves of the artichokes, snap off the stalk and snap away the stem.
2. Spread the leaves apart and dig out the central cone with a teaspoon. Scrape out the choke underneath.
3. Place the artichokes in acidulated water. Heat the oil in a casserole pan and add the artichokes, onion, garlic and white wine and cook for 1 hour.
4. Meanwhile, preheat the oven to 180°C (160° fan) / 350F / gas 4. Cook the lasagne sheets according to packet instructions. Drain and lay out on a work surface.
5. Chop the basil and feta, setting a little aside for the sauce. Spoon the artichoke mixture and feta and basil down one half of each sheet then roll up to form a cylinder.
6. Place in a roasting tin and cover with tomato sauce and sprinkle with reserved feta and basil.
7. Bake for 15 minutes and serve warm.

Rigatoni with Pecorino

500g / 1 lb / 2 cups rigatoni pasta
60g / 2 oz / ¼ cup butter
1 clove garlic, sliced
handful rocket (arugula) leaves, chopped
60g / 2 oz / ¼ cup pecorino
    cheese, grated

1. Cook the pasta in boiling salted water according to packet instructions.
2. Drain, reserving a little of the cooking water and toss in a little butter.
3. Meanwhile melt the butter in a pan with the garlic and when foaming, add the rocket.
4. Stir until the rocket is just wilted, then toss with the pasta.
5. Season and serve with the pecorino sprinkled over.

Three Cheese Orecchiette

500 g / 1 lb / 2 cups orecchiette
200 ml / 6 ½ fl. oz / ¾ cup double
    (heavy) cream
50 g / 2 oz / ⅓ cup Mimolette
    cheese, grated
50 g / 2 oz / ⅓ cup Parmesan, grated
50 g / 2 oz / ⅓ cup Gruyère or
    fontina, grated

1. Cook the orecchiette in boiling salted water according to packet instructions.
2. Warm the cream and stir in the cheeses until they melt.
3. Season generously with black pepper and a little salt.
4. Drain the pasta and toss through the sauce. Serve.

SERVES: **4** | PREP TIME: **5 MINS** | COOKING TIME: **15 MINS**

Orecchiette with Leeks and Gorgonzola

400 g / 14 oz / 4 cups orecchiette
4 tbsp olive oil
1 large leek, trimmed and finely chopped
1 clove of garlic, crushed
50 g / 1 ¾ oz / ⅓ cup pine nuts
200 g / 7 oz / 1 cup gorgonzola dolce
1 lemon, zest finely grated
1 handful micro leaves

1. Boil the pasta in salted water according to the packet instructions.
2. Meanwhile, heat 2 tbsp of the oil in a frying pan and stir-fry the leek for 8 minutes or until soft. Add the garlic and cook for 1 minute, then take off the heat.
3. Reserve a few pine nuts for the garnish and pound the rest with a pestle and mortar. Tip them into a bowl and mash in the gorgonzola, fried leeks and lemon zest. Season with black pepper.
4. Reserve a cup of the pasta cooking water and drain the rest, then return the pasta to the saucepan. Stir through half of the gorgonzola mixture, adding enough of the reserved cooking water to loosen.
5. Divide between four warm bowls and top each one with an extra dollop of gorgonzola, a drizzle of oil and a few micro leaves.

SERVES: 6 | **PREP TIME: 1 HOUR 15 MINS** | **COOKING TIME: 10 MINS**

Deep-fried Ravioli

FOR THE PASTA

500 g / 1 lb 2 oz / 3 ⅓ cups Italian '00' flour

6 eggs

FOR THE FILLING

120 g / 4 oz / 1 cup Gruyère, grated

bunch of rocket (arugula), finely chopped

40 g / 1 ½ oz / ⅓ cup Parmesan, grated

1 egg, beaten

bunch of flat leaf parsley, finely chopped

salt and pepper

vegetable oil for deep frying

1. Place the flour in a bowl and make a well in the centre. Crack the eggs into the well.
2. Using a fork, beat the eggs and then draw in the flour a little at a time until the dough comes together. Knead the dough with your hands for 5 minutes.
3. Cover with film and chill for 30 minutes. Mix together all of the filling ingredients and stir well.
4. Using a pasta machine, roll out the dough into sheets 2mm thick and 10 cm wide. Lay on a floured surface.
5. Place 1 tsp of filling in the middle of the sheet at one end. Repeat all the way along at 5 cm intervals and then brush a little water around each filling in a circle.
6. Place another sheet of pasta on top, then push the sheets together, around each mound of filling. Cut the ravioli into shapes using a knife or a crinkle-edged cutter.
7. Blanch the ravioli in batches in a large saucepan of salted, boiling water for 1 minute before draining well.
8. Heat the oil in a pan and cook the ravioli in batches until golden brown. Drain on kitchen paper and serve.

SERVES: **4** | PREP TIME: **1 HOUR 15 MINS** | COOKING TIME: **5 MINS**

Nettle and Goats' Cheese Tortelli

400 g / 14 oz / 2 ⅔ cups type '00' flour
3 medium eggs
100 g / 3 ½ oz / 4 cups stinging nettle tops, picked with gloves
200 g / 7 oz / 1 cup fresh goats' cheese
1 lemon, zest finely grated
½ tsp freshly grated nutmeg
2 tbsp olive oil
75 g / 2 ½ oz Caprino Romano, in one piece

1. Put the flour and eggs in a food processor and pulse until they form a ball of dough. Knead the dough on a lightly floured surface for 10 minutes, then wrap in clingfilm and leave to rest for 20 minutes.
2. Meanwhile, blanch the nettles in boiling water for 1 minute, then tip into a sieve and squeeze out all the water. Transfer the nettles to a chopping board and chop finely.
3. Mix the nettles with the goats' cheese, lemon zest and nutmeg.
4. Roll out a quarter of the pasta dough and cut it into 10 cm circles with a cookie cutter. Add a teaspoon of the nettle mixture to the centre of each one, then fold in half to enclose. Press firmly round the edge to seal then pinch the two thin ends of the crescent together to make the classic tortelli shape.
5. Repeat three more times to use the rest of the dough and filling.
6. Boil the tortelli in a large pan of salted water for 4 minutes or until the pasta is cooked al dente.
7. Divide the tortelli between four plates. Drizzle with oil then use a vegetable peeler to shave over the Caprino Romano. Season with black pepper and serve immediately.

SERVES: **4** | PREP TIME: **40 MINS** | COOKING TIME: **30 MINS**

Cavolo Nero and Mascarpone Cannelloni

4 tbsp olive oil
2 leeks, finely chopped
2 cloves of garlic, crushed
100 g / 3 ½ oz / 4 cups cavolo nero, stem removed, finely chopped
250 g / 9 oz / 1 ¼ cups mascarpone
200 g / 7 oz / 1 cup ricotta
1 lemon, zest finely grated
2 tbsp basil, chopped
250 ml / 9 fl. oz / 1 cup tomato passata
12 fresh lasagne sheets
75 g / 2 ½ oz / ¾ cup Pecorino Romano, grated
4 sprigs basil

1. Preheat the oven to 190°C (170°C fan) / 375F / gas 5.
2. Heat 2 tbsp of the oil in a large sauté pan and fry the leeks for 8 minutes. Add the garlic and stir-fry for 2 minutes.
3. Add the cavolo nero to the pan and cover with a lid. Cook gently for 20 minutes, stirring halfway through. Tip the mixture into a bowl and mix with the mascarpone, ricotta, lemon zest and basil.
4. Spread the passata in an even layer in a baking dish. Divide the mascarpone mixture between the lasagne sheets and roll them up, then transfer to the baking dish.
5. Cover the dish with foil and bake for 30 minutes.
6. Divide the cannelloni between four plates. Drizzle with the rest of the olive oil, sprinkle with cheese and garnish with basil.

Tagliatelle with Shimeji and Pecorino

400 g / 14 oz tagliatelle
4 tbsp olive oil
2 cloves of garlic, unpeeled, squashed
1 bay leaf
1 strip lemon zest
225 g / 8 oz / 3 cups shimeji
  mushrooms, cleaned
50 g / 1 ¾ oz / ¼ cup butter, cubed
75 g / 2 ½ oz / ¾ cup Pecorino Sardo,
  grated
handful basil leaves

1. Boil the pasta in salted water according to the packet instructions or until al dente.
2. Meanwhile, infuse the olive oil with the garlic, bay and lemon in a large sauté pan until it starts to sizzle. Remove with a slotted spoon, then add the mushrooms.
3. Sauté the mushrooms for 8 minutes or until golden brown and any liquid that comes out of them has evaporated. Add the butter to the pan and shake until it melts.
4. Toss the pasta with the mushrooms and divide between four warm bowls. Garnish with Pecorino and basil leaves.

Linguine with Mozzarella

500 g / 1 lb 2 oz / 2 cups linguine
4 tomatoes, chopped
2 tbsp olive oil
2 tbsp basil, chopped
2 balls mozzarella

1. Cook the pasta according to packet instructions.
2. Meanwhile macerate the tomatoes with oil and salt and pepper and leave for 10 minutes.
3. Once the pasta is drained – not too thoroughly – return to the pan with the tomatoes, chopped mozzarella and torn basil.
4. Toss and serve immediately.

SERVES: 4 | **PREP TIME: 35 MINS** | **COOKING TIME: 5 MINS**

Ravioli with Gorgonzola

500 g / 1 lb 2 oz pasta dough
   rolled into 2 sheets

FOR THE FILLING
10 walnuts
200 g / 7 oz / ¾ cup ricotta
3 tbsp olive oil
4 tbsp parsley, chopped
250 g / 9 oz Gorgonzola, piccante or dolce
2 ripe pears

1. Lightly toast the walnuts in a pan until they start to darken. Place in a food processor and mix to a crumble.
2. Stir into the ricotta with 1 tbsp oil, parsley and seasoning. Lay a sheet of pasta onto a floured work surface and place 1 tsp of the mixture at intervals along the sheet, leaving a 5 cm / 2 in gap between each mound. Brush around each mound with a little beaten egg.
3. Top with the second sheet of pasta and press down lightly around each mound. Cut out or stamp out with a cutter and lay on a baking tray.
4. Warm the serving plates on a low heat in the oven with chopped Gorgonzola so it starts to melt.
5. Slice the pears into quarters and core. Squeeze over a few drops of lemon juice to prevent browning.
6. Cook the ravioli in boiling salted water for 2 minutes, remove and drain on kitchen paper.
7. Toss gently with the melted Gorgonzola and top with the pears.

SERVES: **2** | PREP TIME: **5 MINS** | COOKING TIME: **7 MINS**

Three Cheese Ravioli

500 g / 1 lb / 2 cups ready-made fresh ravioli, such as spinach
   and ricotta or wild mushroom
250 g / 9 oz / 1 cup mascarpone
75 g / 3 oz / ⅓ cup Gorgonzola
50 g / 2 oz / ⅕ cup Parmesan, grated
1 clove garlic, peeled
2 sprigs thyme

1. Cook the pasta in boiling salted water according to packet instructions.
2. Drain, reserving a little of the cooking water and toss with a little oil.
3. Meanwhile heat the mascarpone in a pan with the other cheeses crumbled in.
4. Add the whole garlic clove and thyme, season carefully and stir until the
   cheeses melt.
5. Fish out the garlic and thyme sprigs.
6. Toss the pasta in the sauce and serve.

SERVES: 4 | PREP TIME: 5 MINS | COOKING TIME: 30 MINS

Stuffed Conchiglioni with Brie Cream

2 tbsp olive oil

1 onion, finely chopped

2 cloves of garlic, crushed

100 g / 3 ½ oz / 4 cups Swiss chard leaves, washed

250 g / 9 oz / 1 ¼ cups ricotta

¼ tsp nutmeg, freshly grated

24 conchiglioni pasta shells

150 ml / 5 ½ fl oz / ⅔ cup double (heavy) cream

150 g / 5 ½ oz / 1 ½ cups Brie, rind removed and diced

2 tbsp Parmesan, finely grated

2 tsp cracked black peppercorns

1. Heat the oil in a large sauté pan and fry the onion for 8 minutes. Add the garlic and stir-fry for 2 minutes.

2. Add the chard to the pan and cover with a lid. Let it wilt in its own steam for 4 minutes, stirring halfway through. Tip the mixture into a sieve and squeeze out any excess liquid.

3. Finely chop the chard mixture, then transfer it to a small saucepan and mix with the ricotta and nutmeg. Heat through gently while you cook the pasta.

4. Cook the pasta in boiling salted water according to the packet instructions. Drain well then fill each pasta shell with some of the ricotta mixture.

5. Heat the cream and Brie together until the Brie melts and the sauce starts to bubble.

6. Divide the pasta shells between four plates and spoon over the Brie cream. Sprinkle with Parmesan and cracked black pepper and serve immediately.

Index